MENTAL

TOUGHNESS

Guide to Living a Good Life and Improve
Confidence, Resilience and Mental Toughness
Using Nlp and Emotional Intelligence

(Slow Down the Brain and Be Yourself)

Carol Hardy

Published by Darren Wilson

© **Carol Hardy**

All Rights Reserved

Mental Toughness: Guide to Living a Good Life and Improve Confidence, Resilience and Mental Toughness Using Nlp and Emotional Intelligence (Slow Down the Brain and Be Yourself)

ISBN 978-1-989787-75-5

Legal & Disclaimer

The information contained in this book is not designed to replace or take the place of any form of medicine or professional medical advice. The information in this book has been provided for educational and entertainment purposes only.

The information contained in this book has been compiled from sources deemed reliable, and it is accurate to the best of

or indirectly, of any advice or information presented, whether for breach of contract, tort, negligence, personal injury, criminal intent, or under any other cause of action.

You agree to accept all risks of using the information presented inside this book. You need to consult a professional medical practitioner in order to ensure you are both able and healthy enough to participate in this program.

Table of Contents

Introduction 1

Chapter 1: Self Discipline And Success In Life From A Social

Perspective 5

Chapter 2: Factors That Hamper Self-Discipline............... 17

Chapter 3: What Is Mental Toughness?........................... 39

Chapter 4: Mindset Of A Confident Person...................... 50

Chapter 5: How To Be Mentally Tough 65

Chapter 6: Identifying Bad Habits And Why This Is

Important.. 72

Chapter 7: Transform Negative Energy Into Positive Energy

.... 85

Chapter 8: How To Build Laser Focus.............................. 92

Chapter 9: Mental Toughness & Athleticism 99

Chapter 10: Act Core Principle.. 107

Chapter 11: Improving Your Odds 131

Chapter 12: Business 144

Chapter 13: Mindfulness 147

Chapter 14: The Discipline Of Will And Its Types 157

Chapter 15: Cultivating Mental Toughness Among

Employees.. 175

Introduction

Mental toughness is a going concern among individuals, organizations and nations. It is a very important subject of great reference and with the constant increase in world population and competition, the existence of stiff competition which cuts across every sector of the world economy and business has made it clear that every person who intends to survive must have to learn the rudiments of being a survivor.

It is interesting to know that long age standing discovery of the term "survival of the fittest has come to prove the existence of a common factor that leads to surviving and that is the "fittest". Now the question you should be asking yourself right now is "am I mentally tough enough to fit into the hard situations in the society?"

Mental toughness therefore is not just a topic, it is something that affects every individual in the world today, if you are tough mentally the chances of your survival in the sophisticated and fast developing world is certain. As the population continues to increase and with limited jobs, how do you intend to survive in this information age?

Now is the time for you to look inward and know how you can really become mentally tough. This book is bringing the best pragmatic ways that will show you what you have been missing and what you have not been doing right. I will open up your eyes to the facts and true reality of the nature of the world and you will see what is actually happening.

Then you will be able to determine where you really belong presently, how you can liberate yourself from where you are and graduate or leap to your choice place in life.

You can actually take your destiny into your own hands and chose where to be and when to be and achieve greater heights, mental toughness associates with

2

certain factors and characteristics that will bring out the very best in you when you decide to make a change.

The issues relating to success can be found in people with mental toughness. Hence, successful people are usually mentally tough, there is something that drives them to become very successful, and one of those factors are related to being mentally tough.

Are you having problems in your life? Have you been looking for a way out of your current situation and you are finding it extremely difficult to realize your dreams? Then this book is actually prepared based on vast experience and research.

It will make you to rediscover yourself and become a champion by right and merit.

Nothing comes easy in life except you are born with a silver spoon, and even as at that, you may lost the riches that you have inherited if you don't have the mental toughness or ready to take control of your life, for many have had the opportunity of inheriting great wealth and they are unable to expand with it or manage it well.

Being mentally tough is for both the young and adults.

So take the opportunity provided here and equip yourself for that challenge that comes your way.

Be a different person, stand out from the crowd, be a leader in your area of life and become the champion that you have always dreamed to become, the time is now. Follow the simple steps to become mentally tough to be a survivor and a victorious person. Enjoy!

Chapter 1: Self Discipline And Success In Life From A Social Perspective

Develop Habits of Strong Self-Discipline Right from Childhood

Set up the mechanism

The social importance of building a strong character cannot be stressed enough. Developing self-control is vital for children (Martin Kocher, et al., April 2012). Children with self-discipline and willpower develop into better citizen because they have more control over their minds and thoughts. We begin by setting up the mechanism. But we need to decide the exact point of injection of the self-discipline mechanism. Moreover, we need to see that if such a mechanism for injecting self-discipline were in place, whether it would work effectively. Moreover, we need to ascertain in what ways the motivation for a successful life occurs.

Working of the governing body

First, let us talk about the mechanism of imparting the means to develop self-control. We see that the governing group needs to function as an independent body. This means that children function as separate cognitive units. The parents or the school will not interfere with the functioning of these children other than for providing the basic amenities. The monitoring of the mechanism that imparts and measures the growth of self-confidence in children takes place through another agency specifically appointed for carrying out the task.

Directing children from a social perspective

Children ought to realize the importance of delaying gratification early in life (Martin Kocher et al., April 2012). This will help them develop self-discipline and willpower. Implementing self-discipline in children without looking at any cognitive aspect will impact their academic and health aspects when they grow up. The work that they do and the subsequent economic impact at that point of time depends on the way they develop their self-control today. The pertinent point here is that the adults do not direct the action of the children in an individual manner but act as a collective whole. Being one of the members of the society, they contribute towards providing proper guidance for the children.

Outcome of the self-discipline studies

Studies show that children who had more patience were able to resist habits such as consuming alcohol and smoking cigarettes. These students were leaner, had more willpower and saved more pocket money. They obtained better grades too. When students see the negative impact of impulsive behavior they make them display better delay time with regards to gratification (Romer et al, 1989). High cognitive ability does not always compensate for self-discipline or willpower that is essential for developing technical skills or doing well in school. Self-discipline, the study suggested, played a crucial role in determining beneficial and positive life outcomes.

Understanding The Psychological Aspect of Self-Control

Role of Willpower in Determining Social Interactions

Willpower plays a significant role in any human interaction that does not occur naturally. It covers the entire spectrum of human groups from the shepherd to the business tycoon, the farm laborer to the stock market expert. Surprisingly, it has a profound effect on children since this particular character will produce strong citizens, who will be reliable and produce positive results in society and on the economy. Happiness comes from attaining personal goals and by contributing in a positive way to the society.

From an individualistic point of view, we see that crime, addiction to drugs and domestic violence impact people who do not have the self-discipline or willpower to stay within their camp and do their thing in a proper way. Sexually transmitted disease, debt, prejudice and high rate of drop out from schools happen only to those who lack self-discipline. Overeating and underperformance come from the lack of determination.

Contrasting facet of intelligence

Studies in psychology have unearthed interesting features about intelligence. However, there seems to exist a limit to how much one can increase this intelligence. Learning, therefore, seems to help when you concentrate on things like systematizing the approach. Self-control helps you get into synchrony with the system fast. Therefore, they decided to use their effort to increase the self-control and willpower one has. This seems to work admirably in bettering the standard of human life and adding quality in the form of happiness and peace.

Ration Me Willpower!

Scientists have noticed that willpower is an expendable item. This means that every person has only so much willpower (Kirsten Weir, January 2012). If they spend it on the first task A (say, arranging clothes on hangers), they will have that much less left for the second task B (putting the clothes into the drawer). In a control group experiment, they found that people who develop willpower by doing something that needed their willpower to resist showed better performances. Self-disciplined people who resisted the urge to go for a smoke or a cookie during the break focused on their work better than those who did not resist.

Bottom line on character of citizens

Strong character consists of both the ability to exert self-discipline as well as having 'staying power'. People with a strong character, self-discipline and willpower form the backbone of society. They make all the decisions that become public policies. They dictate the way progress occurs in society. All the segments consisting of bureaucrats, technocrats, working class, the business class, academic community and social organizations benefit from employing people with strong positive social character. Since this part of the character of a citizen begins when they are children, we must put some mechanism in place that will deliver, measure and govern self-discipline and willpower in the children.

Live a Contented and Happy life

Aspects of social control

Social control is an important aspect of the life of a citizen. It reinforces self-discipline and outlines the rules that everyone follows to live a contented and happy life. Social control theory gained prominence at the beginning of the nineteenth century (Ontario Volume 5 Chapter 12). The idea behind social control at that time had its basis on developing self-discipline and social bonds to family, society and school so that deviant behavior does not exist. Friends, teachers, and colleagues helped reinforce this bond developing between them and the students (children). When these bonds break, a crime invariably occurred. There were four main factors that helped society in a huge way. These were **involvement, commitment, attachment and belief**. According to Siegel and McCormick (2006), social control when seen from these four aspects becomes the insulation from criminal entanglement.

Parental attachment plays a dominant role in keeping students on track with progress and personal achievement. In a study of a group of Caucasian males, the report showed that inadequate parental monitoring led students to exhibit violent and deviant behavior. Violence thus could be controlled if one put adequate parental control in place.

Attachment to the school helps student become achievers. It occurs predominantly among those who have self-discipline and willpower. One could see instances of violence and deviant behavior shown by those who did not have an adequate attachment to the school.

Moral and Character Development

To define willpower and self-discipline, one needs to set the sights on the aim that self-discipline leads to. What we will achieve from self-control and determination will show us what we need to do. Primarily, we seek a peaceful and harmonious life. The fundamental step leading to this is education. Education gives you the knowledge that you use to improve your lifestyle. Education has three main aspects to it.

1. Defining the vision of life in that it shows the goals and aspirations of the person
2. Development of character so that the quality of life becomes better
3. Developing the skills required for a satisfactory livelihood

One can understand the character of the person from his or her social conduct.

Character of school students must follow these guidelines:

They must have:
1. Morally sound ethical behavior
2. A standard for personal ideas
3. A sound ethical standard for social values
4. Capacity for discipline

One knows that when one puts sand into a broken bucket, it will seep out. Similarly, a person without the moral fiber to resist temptations will not achieve anything substantial. People without principles will not remain steady in their aims. This will result in poor workmanship. A worker must have the determination to do work perfectly.

To begin with, the person must have an original method for doing things. This type of self-discipline will be the personal stance that one takes when going about their work. We can see the level of commitment from the quality of the output. People who have better self-control will produce superior work. They apply their entire mind to the work all the time they do the work. According to Huitt, W. (2004), the study of this kind of desired outcomes from the children makes it easy to charter their learning programs. It provides the motivation for achieving success in life.

And lastly, one must remain receptive to ideas. Even though one has good moral principles and a high standard of ethics, progress will create changes that do not fit in with your sense of values. This capacity for discipline helps augment social values that exist around you. This is especially necessary for a developing environment which has a lot of new people contributing their share. If you have good self-discipline, you will be able to blend in with everyone. Self-discipline provides the best motivation for success in life.

Chapter 2: Factors That Hamper Self-Discipline

Several factors cause the lack of self-discipline. If you want to cultivate this vital trait, then it pays to learn about the different factors and reasons that could be hampering you from doing so. In this chapter, you will know exactly the specific reasons why you have a hard time cultivating self-discipline. By understanding these reasons and factors, you will know exactly, which you should avoid and overcome. This is the key towards creating a more disciplined and focused version of yourself.

Attitude to your own self, life and to people around you

Some people have a hard time honing self-discipline and control because of their attitude towards their own selves, those around them and their lives. This is the reason why they also find it difficult to be trustworthy, honest, clean and considerate. Avoid viewing your own self, life and those surrounding you as insignificant. Keep in mind that they have their own worth and all forms of life are worthwhile to put your interest, resources, time and energy into. Start seeing life as sacred.

If you want to develop self-discipline, then it's time to change your view of life. Start believing that all forms of life are linked to love. Spend time appreciating and nurturing life. Life is pleasurable and worth loving. Self-control and discipline will instantly arise once you start cultivating your willingness to nurture your own self, those around you and other forms of life.

Lack of self-discipline at home

Another reason why you may have a hard time cultivating self-discipline is because it was not cultivated at home. Your parents are supposed to be your first teachers, and it is in your own home where you should be trained about proper morals, values and discipline. The problem is that a lot of parents at present have less control over their children.

Some countries start to adopt a more modern and liberated culture, so it is no longer surprising if you see children capable of giving their parents a back-off signal in case they feel like their freedom is already threatened. Some parents are also too busy making a living that they no longer have time disciplining their kids and correcting them in case they committed something wrong.

This is the main reason behind the lack of self-discipline in some people. Lack of proper training at home regarding what is right and wrong causes them to grow up with poor discipline.

Lack of awareness

This is another primary reason behind poor self-discipline. Awareness is vital in your own thinking and imagination. Your lack of awareness of the things around you may cause you to be unable to realize that those thoughts that take a huge chunk of your attention are actually negative and have the tendency to damage your overall well-being.

Your negative thoughts, considering the fact that you're unaware of their presence, may feed your consciousness. This hampers your mind power, causing you to spend less time contemplating about what is good for you. Start improving your awareness about those around you, and what is happening in your own thoughts and emotions. If you have a strong sense of awareness, then you know exactly when is the perfect time to practice self-control and discipline, so you can start pulling yourself away from the damaging flow of your thoughts.

Temptations

The temptations around you may also damage your resolve to practice self-discipline. Every day, you will need to deal with various temptations. These include newspaper, magazine and TV ads telling you to buy things. You may also see numerous products that are up for sale in the grocery and department stores.

Other temptations and distractions include some ways to pass time, including TV shows, concerts, movies, restaurants, social media and other forms of entertainment. If you want to make self-control and discipline a part of your system, then it's time to learn about how you can resist these temptations. Avoid following and accepting life's pleasures impulsively. Use common sense when deciding which one is really good for you, to avoid weakening your discipline.

Lack of Inner Strength

Another factor that may prevent you from developing self-discipline is a lack of inner strength. This may worsen if you also have the tendency to laze around, instead of doing things that you need to do. Someone who lacks inner strength, is who tends to avoid doing activities and tasks, especially those that need persistence and effort.

A lot of people favor comfortable laziness than actions that require them to exert effort. Laziness is actually pleasurable and comfortable. It does not require a lot of effort. Self-discipline, on the other hand, requires one to be persistent and to exert effort. It's the main reason why several people have a hard time cultivating discipline.

Passion

What you love or are passionate about often determines what you decide to do. It often has a say on whether you can discipline or control yourself to do what you need to do, or choose your own wants, desires or preferences. That said, it is safe to say that one of the motivating factors in developing self-discipline is love or passion.

However, take note that not everything that you need to do is within your love or passion. This makes it harder to develop self-discipline.

Insignificant goals

This can be linked to your own beliefs. If you set goals that look good, but you believe are not that necessary, then you may have a hard time disciplining yourself to exert effort in achieving them. This is the main reason why you have to look for goals that are really important to you — those that can motivate you to wake up earlier each day, take action on a regular basis and reach them.

If you have insignificant goals, then you may also find it difficult to commit to them. Significant goals, on the other hand, especially those that relate to your passion, drive you to commit to them — so

self-discipline is not that hard to implement.
Lack of self-respect

If you have low self-respect, then you may view the quest to excellence as insignificant. You will never have the willingness and commitment to achieve more than what you attained in the past. How does this relate to self-discipline? The answer is that you need self-discipline to attain excellence, reach your goals, value your reputation in various circumstances and make yourself available to help those in need.

Other factors that could be hampering your desire to develop self-discipline are laziness, material delights and pleasures, ambitions, lack of strict implementation and lack of proper role models. Note that if you don't do something to deal with the mentioned factors, then you may also have a difficult time reaching for what you want to achieve in life. Poor discipline actually has a lot of negative effects not only on you, but also on those around you.

If you don't do something to correct your lack of discipline, then you may be at risk of dealing with the following negative consequences:

- Self-destruction and self-inflicted difficulties
- Lack of responsibility
- Being complacent
- Uncontrollable agitation
- Criticisms, especially those directed to your own self
- Failures

- Grief
- Tendency to let others down
- Lack of self-respect
- Poor health
- Lack of persistence and determination
- Tendency to procrastinate and laze around
- Poor performance

And the list goes on and on. See? Lack of discipline can significantly affect various aspects of your life. Now that you know exactly the specific factors that may have caused you to have a difficult time honing this skill, it will be easier to pinpoint which one you should address. The next chapters of this book aim to help you build discipline by addressing those factors using simple and easy to implement tips.

Basics of Developing Self-Discipline

While there are several qualities that can help you attain success and genuine happiness, one, which guarantees long-term and sustainable effects in various aspects of your life, is self-discipline. This trait is crucial in several areas of your life, including your diet, health and fitness, relationship and work ethics. That said, it is really vital in attaining your goals, practicing a healthier lifestyle and being genuinely happy.

The good news is that self-discipline is a trait that you can learn and hone. You can develop it, provided you practice and repeat it every day. This chapter will focus on some of the most basic tips that you can apply to improve your self-discipline. The good thing about the tips mentioned here is that they can also help you build good habits, get rid of bad ones, and strengthen your self-control just by doing minor changes to your daily routines.

Get Rid of All Temptations

You can easily build self-control and self-discipline if you adhere to the "out of sight, out of mind principle". In this case, it is crucial to get rid of all the distractions and temptations surrounding you. Many consider this as the first vital step in boosting their self-discipline. For instance, if your goal is to take complete control of your eating habits, then get rid of all those foods that are harmful for you in your kitchen. If you don't see unhealthy, processed foods, then you will also less likely to crave them or binge on them.

To boost your focus when you are at work, turn off your mobile phone and eliminate all clutter on your desk. It is also necessary to block sites that may just distract you and consume too much of your time unnecessarily. These include YouTube, Facebook, Twitter and other social media sites.

Though you may have the belief that your willpower is so strong that you can resist even the most captivating distraction, it only takes a while for your weakness to cave in every once in a while, – convincing you to succumb to the temptation. By blocking your access to them, you can easily stop yourself from getting distracted.

Develop the habit of gratitude

In most cases, you are actually spending too much time wanting and desiring things, even those that are not that necessary. By practicing gratitude, it will be easier for you to transition from the habit of constantly wanting more, especially those that you don't have, to appreciate what is in front of you. Doing so will allow you to notice significant improvements in the quality of your life, as well as your level of self-discipline.

Gratitude actually has far-reaching effects. It improves not only your mental and emotional health, but also your spirituality. Aside from that, it easily transitions you from the thought of inadequacy to a state of wealth and abundance. If you always think that you're lacking in something, then focusing on cultivating discipline and attaining your goals will be hard for you.

It's time to stop spending so much of your time and mental capacity thinking and worrying about what you lack now. There's no need to constantly live in the state of fear if you just start to appreciate what you currently have. Note that constantly positioning yourself in a state of lack can result in physical diseases in the long run. It causes stress, which can eventually lead to several harmful diseases.

To practice the habit of gratitude, try to allot ten minutes of your day putting down to writing all the things that you're thankful for. Even in those instances when you feel like there is nothing to be thankful for, you will realize that there is actually something. Put it down into writing, no matter how minor, and you will instantly feel a sense of genuine happiness and gratification.

Meditate

One benefit of meditation is that it aids in putting your mind at ease. It offers a kind of spiritual centeredness, which serves as a means for growth. Through proper meditation, it will be easier for you to cancel out all the unnecessary noises, especially in your mind. Meditation has a huge effect on your ability to practice self-discipline. Since it clears your mind from unnecessary clutter, you can expect it to help set the perfect tone for your entire day.

Meditation also strengthens your physical, spiritual, mental and emotional health. This makes it easier for you to reap its positive effects even if you invest less time and effort. The good thing about meditation is that it does not require you to spend too much time. In most cases, 5 to 15 minutes are usually enough. All it takes it to keep your mind still. Never let it wander.

Bring it back whenever you start to notice that it's starting to wander. Practicing meditation is all about aligning your body with your astral or spiritual being. Through this alignment, you can establish a more focused and happier life since you no longer need to worry about those things that weigh you down. By practicing it regularly, you will notice its ability to lighten your load and enhance your self-discipline.

Set active goals

Active goals are not the same as the other types of goals you set. These are actually the ones that you tend to write down. They are more meaningful, measurable and specific. Since they are active goals, you also need to create an action plan designed to help you attain them. Setting your long-term goals this way makes it easier for you to reach them.

The good thing about an active goal setting is that it helps cultivate self-discipline. It's primarily because of its ability to give you direction. It motivates you to avoid distractions since you can instantly see what you need to do on a particular day. If you don't have active goals, then your life will be lacking in direction.

For you to practice active goal-setting, it's advisable to set long-term goals. Your long-term goals will let you engage in planning on a daily, weekly and monthly basis. You can also keep track of your progress actively. The good thing about this is that it allows you to efficiently perform tracking and analysis. This will let you clearly see your progress – where you are at the present moment and how far you are to your ultimate goal.

You won't also get easily distracted since you can see the results right in front of you. This prevents your subconscious from looking for excuses to delay what you have to do or help in covering up some truths. For active goal-setting to work, make it a point to have daily goals each morning. Find out which among the tasks that you need to do to reach that goal you need to do today. You can then start chasing your goal gradually yet surely.

Chapter 3: What Is Mental Toughness?

"Concentration and mental toughness are the margins of victory" – Bill Russell

Most people have a vague concept of what mental toughness is but often find it quite hard to express it exactly. It is always easy to point to the great athletes of our time, the football players, the runners, the tennis players, the rowers and say "that's mental toughness – look at their success" and that is indeed part of it. However, there is normally far more to it than that. Looking at famous sportsmen and women and reducing mental toughness to that very narrow group of people is wholly counter-productive. It strengthens the feeling that mental toughness is unattainable, that only the tiniest percentage of human beings ever attain mental toughness, that you have to be able to run up and down Everest before you are classified as mentally tough. The next thought process from there is to think, "I'm not a world class athlete. Therefore I can't ever have been or will ever be mentally tough".

Nothing is further from the truth. The simple reality is that everyone can be mentally tough. If you are reading this you are probably already further down the path than most. Never, ever make the mistake of thinking that this is an unattainable goal, that only special people can do it and for some reason you cannot.

Being mentally tough is nothing more than training yourself repeatedly in the correct way, doing the right things at the right time and believing in yourself.

Let me give you one example, just from my own home life, where I have seen mental toughness at its absolute strongest. When I've done that I would like you to think of just one example where you have seen the same thing or even done the same yourself. For now, here is mine.

I come from a family with a brother who is four years older than me. When my brother was 13, he desperately wanted a dog for a pet. He asked my father over and over, he did all the research, he saved up money to help pay for it and pleaded and pleaded and pleaded. My father was initially reluctant. Not so much for financial reasons, but he had a dog when he was younger and he knew how much work was involved. He was primarily concerned with the dog's welfare – Who would walk it? Who would clean it? Who would feed it?

Now my brother was adamant he would do it all. He swore that no matter what he would take the dog out every day. No matter what the weather, no matter how tired he was or if he felt a little low or busy – he would always go for a walk. Every. Single. Day. After a couple of months of this begging my parents relented. We would have the dog. My brother would do the work, but he could have the dog.

The dog came and he was great. He was a terrier, a lovely creature who very quickly became part of the family. For four months my brother was true to his word. He would willingly take him out every day, rain or shine. He fed him, bathed him, took him to the vet – my father paid for everything but he was delighted to see such commitment. After those initial four months however, my brother had other commitments piling up. School work, a part time job, he wanted a greater social life with friends and then girls. His attention to the dog was stretched and he found his time under more and more pressure. He still maintained his efforts though despite the fact he was clearly becoming more and more tired.

After a week or so my father spoke to him. He told him he admired his determination so far and was in many ways delighted to have been proved wrong in doubting his commitment. He was impressed that despite other things competing for his time he had carried on and placed the dog first. He admired my brother's toughness. And then he made him an offer – the two of them would share the burden. They would alternate between them each day the walking and the feeding. Each of them would take on half the responsibility for the dog. This was the deal for the dog to stay. If my brother broke the agreement, if he reneged on his part, the dog would go.

My brother agreed and from that day on the dog never missed a walk. He would go out in the vilest of weather – snow, rain, hail – no matter. The two of them shared the responsibility every day for nine years. They never missed a day.

For me, as an observer, there were two lessons. Firstly, I was impressed by the mental strength to go for an hour's walk even when you might feel exhausted. Even when you might have had a long day at work, hungry and tired, one of them would go out on that walk. That in itself was a really big task. The second lesson was about targets. It was unrealistic for my brother to have promised to do it all and my father knew it. However, he let it go at first, confident in the fact that he believed my brother could and should re-appraise and re-assess regularly.

He believed that when my brother was faced with a target that was difficult but still attainable that he would then push himself to achieve that target and indeed he did, without missing a beat, for years. My father was happy for his part to share the burden out of love for his son and he was happy to take on additional responsibility of his own in order to teach his son about obligation and responsibility. The revised target they agreed between themselves was difficult, very difficult, but there were two critical factors: it was

attainable and the **motivation** was there. More on these factors later.

What mental toughness means

Mental toughness is not about running three marathons in a day. It is something you may well see around you all the time without even realising it. It is the ability to carry on – to persevere even when conditions are difficult and circumstances seem to conspire against you. It is the strength to continue when adversity strikes and to recognise that it inevitably will – that it is how you respond that is important.

It is the strength to set yourself a target that is difficult, but attainable, and to persevere until that target is met. To embrace difficulties and fears and worries and to move through. Mental toughness means you can carry on regardless of the most difficult circumstances you will find yourself in. It means becoming a stronger person and having the confidence to always reach for your goals

Ultimately, it is about finding the right motivation to push yourself beyond what you thought you could manage and still be **confident** that you will succeed. And every single one of us is capable doing that.

Of course, it is one thing to be aware exactly what mental toughness is, but another to be able to acquire it, to nurture it and then to maintain it at the highest level. Over the course of this book I will cover the strategies and techniques you can use every, single day to reach all of your targets through your own strength of will.

Chapter 4: Mindset Of A Confident Person

In this chapter, you will learn:

- The mindset and characteristics of self-confident people

While self-confidence can be a natural trait, that doesn't mean you can't learn to be more self-confident. By analyzing the mindset and actions of naturally self-confident people, you can train yourself to be more like them. With practice, you can rewire your mindset and thoughts so that self-doubt becomes a thing of the past, and self-confidence becomes part of your natural mindset.

The mindset characteristics of self-confident people include:

1. Self-confident people think positively

Life is full of challenges. Every day you are faced with barriers that you need to overcome. Those barriers include things like giving presentations at work, meeting and talking to new people, going to a busy gym – seemingly full of fit, lean people, or confronting a vendor to complain about bad service.

If you think negatively, when faced with challenges, you are already expecting to fail. You expect your presentation to go badly, and subsequently it does. You expect to feel out-of-place at the gym, and subsequently you do. You expect a promotion to go to your colleague, and subsequently it does. You expect the vendor to give you the brush off, and subsequently they do.

Self-confident people expect to be successful, and they expect to win. They expect things to go their way. They don't expect to fail. Words like can't, won't, and don't are not words they use often. Instead, they use words like can, will, and do.

A negative mindset is more likely to produce a negative outcome. Thinking positively means you expect and are more likely to get a positive, favorable outcome.

2. Self-confident people face their fears

Fear takes many forms, and it doesn't always mean there is a risk of physical danger. It could be a fear of failure, fear of rejection, fear of looking silly, or even the fear of not being liked.

People with self-confidence don't let their fears stop them from doing the things they want to do. Instead, they face their fears head-on, or refuse to acknowledge that their fears even exist.

In contrast, someone with low self-confidence is more likely to allow their fears to stop them from doing the things they want to do. For example, if you have a fear of rejection, you may never cross the room and speak to a person you have never met before.

3. Self-confident people take pride in their achievements

Someone with self-confidence will take pride in what they have done. They are more likely to accept praise and acknowledge their role in their achievements. Pride is not bragging. It's merely acknowledging the feeling of satisfaction and pleasure that comes from one's achievements.

In contrast, someone lacking self-confidence is likely to attribute any successes to luck, or the generosity of others. They are less likely to take pride in or responsibility for their achievements.

4. Self-confident people look after themselves

Self-confidence comes from within. You need to be happy with yourself. If you are not, it's very unlikely that you will feel self-confident. Most self-confident people take time to look after themselves. They exercise to make sure they are fit and healthy, they dress well, are well-groomed, and they have good posture.

If you are unfit, look untidy or unclean, or constantly slouch, you will not feel happy or confident. But, if you change these things, your self-confidence will improve almost automatically. If you LOOK self-confident, you are more likely to FEEL self-confident, and others will assume you ARE self-confident.

5. Self-confident people believe in themselves

Self-confidence and self-belief go hand in hand. Self-confident people intrinsically believe things like:

Yes – I am the right person for the promotion.

Yes – I do have a good business idea.

Yes – I can meet those deadlines.

Yes – I do deserve that pay rise.

Yes – People do enjoy my company.

The opposite of belief is doubt and you will notice in life that self-doubt will make self-confidence much harder to come by.

6. Self-confident people know what they want to achieve

Most self-confident people have a plan. They know what they want from life and how to achieve it. They are usually good goal setters, good planners, and good at doing whatever needs to be done to achieve those goals. Those goals can be work, health, finance, or relationship-based but self-confident people know what they want from life and how they are going to get it.

7. Self-confident people lift other people up rather than knock them down

Self-confident people do not knock other people down to feel good about themselves. They don't belittle their colleagues. They are not bullies, and they do not fear competition, alternative views, or criticism.

Instead, people with self-confidence want to help the people around them, as well as themselves. Self-confidence should be infectious and benefit everyone. Lack of self-confidence often shows up as unpleasant behavior toward others, especially if those people are deemed to be more successful.

8. Self-confident people learn from their mistakes

Something in the nature of human consciousness prevents us from being self-confident if we keep making the same mistakes over and over again. But even self-confident people make mistakes. In fact, because they are often prepared to take more risks, they may even fail more often than they succeed! However, where a less confident person will probably quit after failing, someone with self-confidence will get back up, dust themselves off, and start all over again, learning from their mistakes in the process.

9. Self-confident people are determined to succeed

It doesn't matter how many times you get knocked down, it's how many times you get back up that matters. Self-confident people are prepared to keep on trying until they succeed. Success can take years, but if you have self-confidence, you are much less likely to quit – especially when the going gets tough. Self-confident people have the determination to keep on slogging away to reach their goals.

10. Self-confident people have positive body language

Self-confidence might be a mindset, but it effects how you look too. Self-confident people use positive body language to exude confidence. Eye contact, good posture, easy but genuine smiles, voice tonality and pitch, and positive language all suggest self-confidence.

These traits are a sort of chicken-and-egg situation. If you have self-confidence, you will look self-confident. But, if you look self-confident, you will also feel self-confident. As the saying goes, fake it until you make it!

11. Self-confident people expect to succeed

This is something we've already touched on in the first characteristic but there is a subtle difference between positivity and expectation to succeed. Whereas positivity is more about feeling hopeful or optimistic about current situation and life in general, an expectation to succeed has a different flavor of intent to it. It can be felt a bit more deeply when one is taking the right action towards their goals. For example, it manifests as the "butterflies in your stomach" when you're approaching or being approached by a romantic partner as opposed to a stranger. If you have self-confidence, you expect things to go your way. You expect to be successful, and you expect to win. When faced with any kind of challenging situation, in your mind, it's already in the bag. That doesn't mean your win will come easily. Instead, you expect your effort to pay off.

12. Self-confident people absorb set-backs positively

Of course, even if you have lots of self-confidence, there will be times when things don't go your way. Your team might lose, your business might fail, or your relationships might break up. Someone with plenty of self-confidence will get up, dust themselves off, and get back on track despite their apparent failure. Mistakes and failure can be very positive. People with self-confidence treat set-backs as valuable learning opportunities. They are able to stay grounded in the face of adversity.

Chapter summary:

Some people are born with self-confidence, while other people need to develop it. Whether it's already built-in or something they developed, self-confident people share a number of traits. Even if you aren't naturally self-confident, you can learn and develop the mindset of a self-confident person.

Chapter 5: How To Be Mentally Tough

Mental toughness is difficult to achieve. It takes constant training and exercise to train one's mind and body to be strong altogether. It is not enough to be strong. One has to remain strong all throughout to be considered mentally tough. On top of that, such strength should result in victory or achievement.

So how can you be mentally tough?

1. Train your mind to be tough: The human mind is a spectacular system. It is very powerful—more powerful than anyone can ever imagine. The mind has the ability to achieve what it can conceive. If you want to be mentally tough, then you have to train your mind to be tough. Change the way you think and perceive things. If you are on the verge of giving up, do not let negativity hamper your desire to achieve your goals and finish what you have started. Your mind can be tough if you feed it constantly with positive thoughts and encouraging words. Believe in yourself and your abilities. Always think that you can do anything even if you are not sure about that yourself. It is easier for you to achieve something if you condition your mind that you will definitely reach it. Don't give up easily.

2. Train your mind to focus: Focus is the driving force to being mentally tough. If the person is easily distracted, nothing will be done. Focus is very important to get the job done. In order to train your mind to focus, you have to know what you want. Set your expectations and your goals and determine if the goals are in line with your abilities and interest. It is easier to focus on something that really interests you. When you have set your goal, devote time to perfect your craft. It will never happen overnight, but if you have focus, you will be able to exert more effort and become better at what you do much sooner than you expected.

3. You have to believe in your ability: Mentally tough people believe in themselves and they know what they are capable of. They don't need other people to inspire them because they are empowered to give their best shot at everything they do. Mentally tough people know their limitations as well and they strive harder to improve on them. They don't give up easily and they work hard to achieve their goals. When you know what you want and if you are clear about the things that matter to you, it is very easy to strive towards that direction. Optimism is the key. For example, who would have thought that the highest mountain on Earth will be conquered by many people? It only takes one person to believe in himself and he was able to empower a lot of other people to do the same. When you believe you can do something, you will.

4. Mind control: Control is a distinct component of mental toughness. It is not only the mind that can be controlled but the emotions as well. People who are mentally tough can exhibit extraordinary control over their emotions and they manage to keep their cool even when the situation is not favorable to them. Keep your mind focused and don't let negative emotions overcome you. Fill your mind with positive thoughts and look for positive things that are beyond what's happening. Try to rationalize. Understand the situation, this way you will be able think calmly and decide what is the best thing to do in that situation. It will help if you relax your mind a bit. If your head is in turmoil you will not be able to control it. Take some time off your busy schedule and try to do something fun and productive at the same time like crossword puzzle, Sudoku, chess, board games or read a good and relaxing book.

5. **Don't give in to anxiety:** Anxiety leads to many negative things and can harm your health. Try to avoid anxiety by avoiding stressful situations. Learn to cope with stress and do not overwork yourself. Learn to be punctual and be organized. Expect the worst but hope for the best. Here's how you cope with anxiety:

a.Take deep breaths to help you calm down

b.Breathe in through your nose and exhale through your mouth

c.Count 1-2-3 while inhaling and 1-2-3 while exhaling

d.Feel your stomach expand rather than allowing your chest to rise and fall.

6. **Face your fears**: Mentally tough individuals have nothing to be afraid of. Fear is only in the mind. Danger is real but it is not a reason for you to be afraid of everything. If you are tough, you will face your fears and overcome them. Phobia for example is an irrational fear of something. The only way to cure this is when you expose yourself to these elements and only then will you realize that there is really no reason to be scared of them. Bad

memories can be replaced with good ones. Try to associate these things with good things that happened and you will be able to overcome your fear. It is never easy of course but it takes careful and constant practice to eradicate fears. If you want to be mentally tough, you have to be bigger than your fears. Professional help is needed in extreme cases but in more common cases, fears can be easily conquered.

7. Step out of your comfort zone: The world is full of adventures and excitement and only the confident and mentally active are able to explore. Mentally tough people are always on the go and so they discover a lot of interesting things around them. They learn new things. Try different sports, eat different cuisines, travel to other countries, and venture to deeper waters and meet new people. Mentally tough enjoy their life more than those who are reserved and unwilling to leave their comfort zones. If you want to live a healthy lifestyle and be able to overcome the challenges that come your way, you have to see the world in a different light. The only way to do that is when you go out of your comfort zone and explore! Only then will you realize that the world is a much better and interesting place that you have ever imagined it would be. When your views of the world become positive, your mind will be tough and positive as well. Only then will you overcome the hardships you will be facing. You will eventually be able to strive harder to achieve your goals because you know that the world is not so bad after all, that everyone has a place to be, and that success is not at all elusive.

Chapter 6: Identifying Bad Habits And Why This Is Important

Every person has bad habits. This is inevitable, and a part of life. However, once you have awareness of the habits that are negatively impacting in your life, you can start to make the necessary changes to reverse them and replace them with habits that are beneficial. The first step is being able to determine which of your habits are bad. Once you do this, you want to make note of them, and start following the process necessary to get rid of the habits and their negative consequences.

How to Identify Bad Habits

What causes bad habits in the first place? Pinpointing the source of poor habits will help you to not only curb them now, but curtail forming them later. The following are common causes of bad habits:

- Boredom and stress
- Seeking gratification
- Your environment
- Individual needs
- Your peers

Here are a few steps you want to take to identify and evaluate your bad habits.

1. Write down all of the habits you have that you feel could be having a negative impact on your self-discipline and ability to reach your goals.

2. Be specific about the impact that these bad habits are having on your life. Make sure that you are honest, and that you write down in full, specific details what the negative consequences are.

3. Consider and write down how any of your habits might be affecting other people around you. This may help you to uncover how certain habits are bad, even though you might not personally feel their negative impact.

You may also ask yourself these questions regarding each of your habits to determine if a specific habit is bad or not:

- Is the habit making it harder for you to reach any goals?
- Is the habit causing you to experience negative feelings?
- Is the habit making you feel guilty?
- Is the habit negatively affecting other people besides you?

If you said "yes" to any of these, the habit is most likely a bad influence that needs to be replaced with something that is good.

The Importance of Replacing Bad Habits

Now you have learned about what it takes to replace the bad habits in your life, so the next step is to determine what the positive effects will be. Once you see the immense benefits of replacing bad habits, it will make it easier to create a replacement plan and stay on track. Remember that you learned in a previous chapter that changing your mindset can contribute to easily altering your bad behaviors and thoughts.

When you replace the habits in your life that are bad with good ones, it can do the following:

- You will find it easier to reach your immediate goals
- You will find that the foundation of your life is more stable and more conducive to achieving success

- You will be able to reduce, or even eliminate, how much time you waste each day
- You can more easily create a life plan that allows you to develop reasonable long-term goals
- You can develop good habits that allow you not to have to rely on daily or hourly motivation to get things done
- You will often find yourself in a better mood with stronger mental health overall
- You can take control of your health
- It is easier to form relationships that are strong and positive
- You will be able to better manage your time and not be late

- You will find that it is easier to manage your personal finances

Just make sure that the good habits you do develop are actually good for you. For example, getting more sleep is usually a positive change, but if you are getting too much, it can actually be another bad habit. The key is ensuring that the good replacement habits are within a good balance for your life and goals.

Techniques to Replace Bad Habits with Good Habits

This section will focus on common bad habits and the techniques that you can use to replace them. You likely have at least a few of these habits, so it is important to know about them and the work you need to do to eliminate them and their consequences from your life.

You eat when you are not hungry.

There are several ways to stop this habit. First, you can plan your meals and snacks. Create a meal schedule to follow each day. Next, literally ditch the junk food from your kitchen, and make sure what you are eating is healthy. Third, make sure that you are actually feeling hunger before you eat. Lastly, do not continue eating after you feel full.

You watch too much television.

Set a limit on how much television you are going to watch each day. The maximum should be two hours. Next, schedule activities to get you out of the house, doing something more active to occupy your time. Alternatively, take up a hobby that will get you out from in front of the television when you have free time at home.

You spend too much money.

It is great to buy yourself something nice on occasion, but you want to balance your spending, or else you can find yourself in immense debt. Start by exploring your finances so that you can see where you are spending. Create a budget of your fixed, variable, necessary, and unnecessary expenses. Next, see where you can make cuts. For example, do you have multiple digital television subscriptions? Start by cutting out at least one. Craft a schedule for *when* you can indulge, versus when to stick strictly to your budget.

You drink too much alcohol.

Most people don't have a problem with the occasional drink, but if you find yourself enjoying several cocktails most evenings, it is time to make a change. Start by evaluating how much you are actually drinking and how much money it costs you. This will make it easier to cut down. Next, choose two days a week when you can have a drink, and make sure that on these days you have no more than two.

You use tobacco products.

This is a habit you want to eliminate completely because of the risks to your health, and it can be difficult due to the element of nicotine addiction. It is best to talk to your doctor. They can help you to determine if a medication might be helpful, or if substitution or cold turkey is the best solution for you.

Chances are, you still have some habits on your list that were not included above. The following process can be applied to any bad habit that you are trying to break:

- Identify the reason you have or began the bad habit
- Make the conscious decision to address the habit; you can not just ignore it after identifying the habit, because it will not just disappear without work
- Record the details of your habit, including the cue and why you enjoy it
- Write down why you want to quit the habit (do not focus on what you will lose by quitting the habit, but what you will gain once it is gone)
- Tell yourself frequently that you are going to quit it
- Prepare and plan for challenges and mistakes
- Change your environment or prepare with alternative actions, to make it so

there is no room for the bad habit anymore

- If possible, find a friend who is working to lose same bad habit and keep each other accountable so you can both work to eliminate it from your lives
- Forgive yourself if you slip up; it can take time to break a bad habit, and this is okay, as long as you regain your focus and keep working toward breaking it

Chapter 7: Transform Negative Energy Into Positive Energy

Stop Complaining

Complaining doesn't serve any purpose. Rather, it actually fuels the negative energy in a room and keeps it going for far longer than it needs to. Complaining doesn't solve anything; rather, it merely lets the people around you know how unhappy you are. Your bad mood quickly spreads to those around you, infecting them like a virus.

Instead of complaining, try offering solutions to the problems that you see. Maybe some problems are intractable, but that doesn't mean that all problems are. Perhaps you can see at least a partial solution that, when implemented, will make the problem more manageable. Offering a solution will quickly change the energy in the room for one of the negativity associated with complaining to the positivity of knowing that you are doing something to help solve the problem with which you are being faced.

Accept What You Can't Change

There are a lot of things that we can't control. We can't control the weather, the actions of others, the economy, climate change, the price of a gallon of milk, or any number of things that affect our daily lives. However, we can change our reactions to these things. Do you respond with negativity and complaining, thereby fueling the negative feedback loop of despair and hopelessness? Or do you respond with a positive, can-do attitude that is ready to meet the challenges that you are facing? By changing the way that you respond to events, you can actually change the outcome!

Be Aware of Your Surroundings

Know what is going on in the world around you. Know what the current events in the news are, what challenges your company is facing, and what conflicts need to be settled. Then, after you are aware of what is going on, turn off the news. Don't feed into the emotions surrounding the conflicts that need to be resolved. Instead, being armed with the facts of the situations, make a plan for success. Set a goal and take measurable steps to achieve that goal.

Get Rid of Energy Vampires

Energy vampires are people who suck all of the positive energy out of a room. Some energy vampires are what psychologists call emotional vampires — they drain all of the emotional energy out of a person, then come back for more. Don't allow those people to dominate your life. You can't avoid them completely, but you can minimize the influence that they have on you.

Develop some techniques to limit the time that you spend with people who drain you of your energy. Maybe when you see an energy vampire approaching, you can immediately focus on your task. When that person starts to talk to you in such a way that you feel robbed of energy, politely tell him or her that you are busy and can't talk at the moment. Maybe if an energy vampire approaches you and starts complaining incessantly, you could tell him or her that you will be happy to discuss solutions but you are trying to eliminate complaining from your life.

Surround Yourself With Positive People

Along the same lines of getting rid of energy vampires is replacing the negative people in your life with positive people. Some people are irreplaceable, like your boss, co-workers, or family members.

However, you can take steps to limit the negative influence that those people have on you. Perhaps you could have a conversation with your boss or spouse about how you are trying to improve yourself and see if he or she is willing to help you stay on plan rather than berate or demean you when you fall short. Perhaps your children could benefit from seeing you try to stay positive, and you could enlist them as accountability partners to help you stay on track.

People, like drinking buddies, who you only see occasionally for a night out on the town, can probably be easily replaced. Find new friends who want to see you become the best person that you can be and will infuse you with their positive energy to help you make the changes that you are trying to make.

Practice Zoom Focusing

Zoom focusing is when you shut out all distractions so as to pay attention to exactly what needs to be done, whether that is improving your performance at work, building a better family life, exercising more frequently, or whatever needs to be done to improve your life. Put a "No Distractions Allowed" sign up inside your brain to remind you that you are trying to focus on exactly what you need to do to move on with your life and get ahead.

Chapter 8: How To Build Laser Focus

Brad Paisley, an American country music singer-songwriter once said, "If you make the mistake of looking back too much, you aren't focused enough on the road in front of you."

Killer focus is crucial to making sure that clutter, temptations, and distractions do not affect you, and that you remain dedicatedly committed to your goal (s). Distractions take many forms and can annoy you in unimaginable ways. They can be the negative talk of the naysayers around you, your inner temptations that lure you towards meaningless tasks, or your urge to give in to an adversity. These things debilitate your confidence and to focus on your goal, you must become capable of overcoming these distractions. Here are some tips and strategies that will help you do that:

#1: Get enough sleep

This one is a no-brainer: if you do not sleep enough, you will forever struggle with staying focused on your goals and performing optimally to achieve them. According to the National Sleep foundations, to think rationally, have good cognitive abilities, and to focus better on tasks, adults need an average of 7 to 9 hours of sleep. If you do not sleep well and adequately, this may be the reason why you feel distracted throughout the day.

Set a specific sleep time and sleep at the exact time every single day. You may toss and turn for a few days, but do not give in to the temptation to get out of bed, stay put; you will eventually settle in to the new timings.

Make sure you switch off your phone at least an hour before going to bed as the blue rays emitted by screens messes up your circadian rhythm, the biorhythm that manages your natural sleep cycle.
#2: Try the ABC method

A good technique you can use to overcome distractions is the ABC method, an acronym for being **Aware, Breathing** deeply, and then **Choosing** your options.

Every time you feel distracted, become more aware of what you are doing and your aim for doing it, take a few deep breaths for about 5 minutes and when you feel calmer, choose what you need to do. When you feel calmer, you think better and are likely to make the correct decision.

#3: Stop Multitasking

Multitasking is one of the biggest enemies of focus to date. When you multitask, you make more mistakes than you would make if you worked on one task at a time. Switching between tasks hampers your focus as you do not allow yourself time to understand and adjust to one task. This confuses you and makes you perform poorly, which only reduces your productivity.

To keep this from happening, stop multitasking especially when it comes to high priority tasks. When working on an important task, become aware of what you are doing and consciously take each step at a time. Immerse yourself in the process so that you enjoy it more and do it with keen interest. This also improves your focus and productivity, which helps you yield desired results.

#4: Keep something green and red in your work environment

A study determined that looking at something green for 40 seconds while taking a quick break from work improves your ability to focus. Another study conducted in 2009 showed that those who look at colour red when working on a task focus better on it and have an increased attention to detail.

To benefit from the positive effects of these colours, keep a plant or two or some other things that are green in colour in your office, and have a few red objects or pieces of visible decor. Every time you take a quick break, look at a green or red object so that your focus improves.

#5: Drink Coffee

Research shows that about 2 cups of coffee a day provide you with just the right amount of caffeine you need to feel alert and focused. Therefore, you can take a nice cup of coffee before you start your important task and then have another cup at midday to boost your focus.

#6: Take breaks

When working on long, complicated tasks break them down into smaller parts and take breaks in between the accomplishment of the smaller bits of the larger task. For instance, if you have worked on a task for an hour, take a 15-minute break to relax, regain your focus, and refresh your spirits. This helps you get back to the task with increased focus and you end up doing it well.

If you dedicatedly work on these tactics, you will quickly build laser focus. This will consequently improve your level of discipline and your productivity. To boost your productivity further, employ the tactics discussed in the next chapter.

Chapter 9: Mental Toughness & Athleticism

As previously stated in Chapter 1, mental toughness does not have a clear-cut or definite definition. Mental toughness may mean something different for each individual, however most folks have the same notion. When applied to sports and athletics, mental toughness is a term that is most often used in order to describe an athlete's mental state as he or she faces multiple sport-related challenges. Athlete's benefit from mental toughness in both competition and practice settings as a personal quality that allows them to persevere through challenges in order to succeed in their sport of choice.

American author, journalist, and reporter Charles Duhigg was quoted stating: "Your brain has to decide what deserves attention and what deserves to be ignored, and the way it does it is compare what we expect is going to happen to what's actually going on." Duhigg describes mental toughness as the practice of training your brain to only pay attention to what is truly important while simultaneously blocking out or ignoring negative and useless information that will just clutter your mind space.

Jesse Owens was a well-known American athlete in the United States of America during the 1930s. Owens was an African American track and field star who succeeded in setting multiple records for his sport before traveling to Germany as part of the American team for the 1936 Olympic Games. During the time of the 1936 Olympic Games, Germany was being ruled by the Nazi regime and even tried to prevent Jewish athletes as well as athletes of color from participating in the games (in an event to show that the Aryan race were superior to other races). The American Olympic team, however, featured numerous African American athletes and won six Olympic gold medals thanks to African Americans. Jesse Owens won four of these Olympic gold medals while representing America and also broke two Olympic world records during the 1936 Olympic Games. Jesse Owens faced multiple instances of backlash and racial hate while competing in America (America was still overcoming issues relating to segregation at the time), though these instances were minimal compared to what he faced in competing in the 1936 Olympic Games. While most were accepting of African American athletes after the games had begun, these athletes faced a lot of stress and pressure before the games in trying to find out if they would even be allowed to compete because of their racial background. While facing racial inequality and having to wonder if he would even be allowed to compete in the 1936 Olympic Games, Jesse Owens had to continue in training and competing in his sport. In order to successfully train for the Olympics despite all the external pressures he faced,

Owens demonstrated an immense amount of mental toughness in his ability to block out these pressures as well as overcome numerous obstacles that stood between him and Olympic gold. Thanks to Owens' natural athletic ability, talent, mental toughness, and willpower; he was able to not only participate in the 1936 Olympic Games but return home a champion and American track icon.

Melissa Dahl is a blogger for *Science of Us* and writes "Those who keep it together under pressure are storytellers, essentially. They narrate their own lives to themselves--things that have just happened, things that are about to happen. They daydream about the day ahead and review the hours that have already passed. In doing this, scientists argue, they learn how to best direct their attention and are better at choosing where to focus and what to ignore." Dahl's statement illustrates the belief that you are more likely to become successful in achieving your goals if you condition your mind to visualize yourself overcoming challenges that you may face along the way. Melissa Dahl's statement also summarizes that this mental discipline is able to help your brain stay on the right track to achieve your personal or professional goals rather than allowing yourself to get distracted by small obstacles. Think of it this way: if you allow your brain to view a pebble as a mountain, then it may as well be a mountain (and wouldn't you rather step over a pebble than climb a mountain?). Believe that these external stressors are small and insignificant so that you are able to tackle them easily. Many athletes find success in this belief and are constantly driven to be better by the challenges they face regularly. When an athlete sees a challenge or a situation that is essentially telling them that they can't accomplish something, they do not shy away from a fight. Athletes take on every challenge with fiery dedication and say "watch me" before overcoming the exact obstacle that stands between them and success. This extreme sense of willpower and mental toughness is a personal characteristic that allows them to continuously achieve their goals and become successful.

Vince Lombardi has coached dozens of athletes to success. As a former NFL football coach who has lead players to the NFL championships as well as multiple Super Bowls, Mr. Lombardi knows what it takes to make a football player an incredibly successful athlete. Lombardi has credited mental toughness as being an essential asset to athletes multiple times, and shows this belief in the following quote: "Mental toughness is essential to success."

Chapter 10: Act Core Principle

This skill teaches about perceiving things as they are, without any bias or judgment.

People often see images, thoughts, events, memories, thoughts and similar cognitions from a subjective point of view. Their perceptions are heavily influenced by their personal emotions, past experience, values, bias and similar subjective feelings. This subjectifies can alter perception so much that something neutral becomes either severely positive or negative.

Take the object "chocolate". Say chocolate to a group of people and every one of them reacts or sees in very different ways.

Chocolate in itself is a neutral object. Perceptions influenced by personal feelings, experiences and biases turn it into something else.

To someone who loves chocolate, the word alone may be enough to call up memories of silky smooth sweet treat. This may already make the person start to drool and remember all the delicious chocolate tasted in the past and anticipate the same in the near future.

For a diabetic, the word "chocolate" may cause 2 possible feelings. One, it can produce a bittersweet feeling. The person may recall the chocolates eaten in the past and longs to have another at that moment but realizes that the diabetes condition might worsen if that urge is satisfied. Hence, the memory of the chocolate experience may cause a positive perception but invoke negative (i.e., sadness) emotion because of the current health condition.

On the other hand, another diabetic may have purely negative perception of the word chocolate. The first thoughts that come to mind might be all the negative experiences of being a diabetic. Hence, the chocolate is now viewed as a negative stimulus.

For a dieter, the word chocolate may be viewed as negative because of the calories. For a mom, it may also be viewed as a negative stimulus because it is something that she wants her young children to avoid eating too much of. Someone currently nursing a toothache may see this stimulus as something to avoid.

For a sad person, the word chocolate may be somewhat uplifting because it is the go-to binge food that helps make him/her feel better. For a chocoholic, the word alone may start intense cravings for it.

There are so many other reactions that different people may have with just a single neutral stimulus. All these are not because of the inherent characteristics of the stimulus but because of the positive or negative perception of the stimulus. These varying perceptions are influenced by so many factors, such as past experience with the stimulus, present relationship with the stimulus, feelings, and so on.

Most of the time, these influenced perceptions can distort reality. This distortion becomes the source of internal stress and negativities that in turn, affect behavior and mindset.

Cognitive defusion seeks to equip an individual with capabilities to see things as they are rather than what they appear to be. This skill seeks to help a person to take things as mere objects- thoughts as thoughts, images as images, words as bits of language.

For example, cognitive defusion equips a person to listen to a statement "I am not good enough" as mere words. Whenever this negative self-belief pops into mind, cognitive defusion can be applied to keep it from negatively affecting thoughts, perception and behavior.

How to apply cognitive defusion

Essentially, cognitive defusion involves a set of mental activities and thinking strategies that reduces impact of unwanted, distressing thoughts. This skill reduces the impact, not seeking to entirely eradicate the negative impact. Realistically, nothing can be totally eradicated. Another thing is that negative thoughts, if properly managed, can also exert some positive effects on a person. For example, the statement "You are not good enough" can lower self-esteem. If this self-belief is properly managed, this statement can be used as a motivation to improve one's self.

Cognitive defusion works by altering stimulus function. "Stimulus" is the negative thought and "function" is the emotional impact, associated pain, invoked negative emotions, believability and related cognitive processes.

There are 2 main ways for individuals to deal with negative self-thoughts:

1. See the negative thoughts as facts, judgments, remarks and opinions about the self.

2. See the negative thoughts as mere words, feelings and sensations.

Words used for our thoughts become a person's internal narrative. Applying cognitive defusion seeks to change that internal narrative. It alters the context of these internal narrative instead of changing the thoughts. It seeks to distance and dissociate the self from these thoughts. It can be like taking an observer stance to the thoughts instead of an active participant.

This can help in reducing both the believability of the negative thoughts and the emotional distress these can cause. Cognitive defusion as a skill is about changing the mindset from "You are what you think" into "You are having these thoughts" and "You are observing these thoughts". It turns "I am unworthy" thoughts into "I am having thoughts of being unworthy".

At this stage, it may seem like a play at semantics, merely rearranging words. However, this simple rearranging of words can already have a huge impact on self-esteem and self-confidence, as well as outlook in life.

The change in approach to negative thoughts gives the person the needed distance in order to reduce the emotional distress caused by these thoughts.

Another thing to understand about cognitive defusion is that it involves acceptance of these thoughts. Does that mean you accept you are unworthy or incapable? NO.

It means accepting that you have THOUGHTS of being unworthy or incapable. What difference does this make? This change means you acknowledge that you have doubts about yourself, that you have negative thoughts about yourself but you do not feel the negative emotional impact of these thoughts because you see as thoughts only not a fact about yourself.

The cognitive defusions is about changing the thoughts in order to create a distance between these thoughts and the self to reduce the negative impact on thoughts, emotions and eventually, self-esteem and self-confidence. It's about allowing negative thoughts to come and go as they are without allowing these to leave a significant mark on your being.

It is NOT changing negative self-beliefs but changing the RELATIONSHIP to these beliefs. One way to see this is instead of letting yourself drown in water of negative beliefs, you learn to swim in it and go on with life.

Techniques for cognitive defusion

To distance the self from the negative thoughts, here are some helpful techniques to use:

1. Reframe the thought

One simple way to cognitively defuse negative thoughts is to reword the thoughts. Instead of "I am not capable of doing this task", reword it into "I'm having thoughts of not able to accomplish this task". This takes the self away from the core of the negative thought and making the thought as an entirely separate object from the self.

2. Treat the thought as something playing in the radio

You can treat these negative thoughts as merely sound from a radio playing in the background. Notice when you are playing the radio. You have times when you are really focusing on what is heard from the radio. Then at times, your mind treats the radio as just something in the background.

Use this same response consciously when dealing with your thoughts. You can use your imagination to help things along. Once you start thinking negatively about yourself, such as "I look fat and boring in this dress", you envision a radio playing in the background. The radio is playing the statement "You look fat and boring in that dress". The impact makes a huge difference when you hear the statement and when you declare to yourself that you are that statement.

By envisioning the statement as playing from a radio in the background, will yourself into tuning off that radio. You can imagine yourself turning the volume down and focus on the greater task in reality- whether getting through a meeting or taking an active, positive part at a party.

3. Acknowledge and move on

This is similar to reframing a negative thought about yourself. A lot of negative thoughts are automatic. These come from the subconscious and developed over years of experiences. Many things have happened in the past that reinforced these thoughts.

At this point in your life, you take a different approach to these automatic negative thoughts. Treat these thoughts as coming from a part of the mind and it is not the entire mind. It is just one thought among many others and this thought is just a thought and not your entire being.

4. Write it down

Writing the negative thoughts is another way of giving it a separate form. This physical form helps the mind to treat it is just an object, among so many. This form also helps the mind to acknowledge the thought and then treat it as a separate object or stimulus.

For example, write down a negative self-belief "I am an incapable person". By writing it down, look at it and see it as a separate object. It is a written statement. It is not your entire being.

5. Read the statement/s repeatedly

After writing down the negative thought, read it over and over. While reading, be mindful of your emotional response. Most often, the intensity of its emotional effect on you should diminish, even dissipate.

This technique is called Titchener's Emotional Word Repetition Strategy. Emotionally negative self-thoughts are often attached to specific beliefs, judgment, feeling or object. These anchors act as a starting for an ever-growing cycle of negative self-thoughts and increasingly painful emotions. These are caused by biased implications and emotional interpretations based on these anchors.

For example, many people suffer from low self-esteem because of self-belief that they are "ugly and fat". These are two short words that can trigger a snowballing of negative thoughts and painful emotions to the point that the person no longer finds happiness in life. "Ugly and fat" becomes anchors subject to biased and emotional interpretations.

"I did not get the job I wanted because I am ugly and fat." "I'll never find someone who will truly love me because I am ugly and fat." "I'll live and die alone, with no one to love because I am ugly and fat." "I will have to work harder because no one will be there to take care of me."

And so on.

The string of negativities will continue just because of two simple words. There may be some truth to these negative thoughts, most often very little but their existence are intrusive.

Using Titchener's strategy involves writing or just saying the emotionally-weighted word/s several times. Repetitions are often quick, as many as possible within 30 seconds. Say the words, loud, consistently and clearly.

The scientific basis of this is the process called reactive inhibition. Repeated stimuli such as words match repeated neural firing. Repeated firing of neurons of the same type tends to diminish the effects or the potency of that neural pathway. Just think of doing the same things over and over and in time, you lose interest in it.

With forced repetition on specific neural firing, as in Titchener's Strategy, triggers an inherent neural response to reduce that firing and eventually cause it to stop. Hence, forced repetition of emotionally-charged negative statements will result in repeated neural firing that triggers inherent neural response of diminishing the effects and eventually causing the reaction to that specific stimulus to stop.

6. Classify the negative thoughts

Study the negative thought you have written down. Is it an evaluation or a description. Most often, negative thoughts are evaluations. The evaluations are often painful and comes from within and not from the world.

For example, the negative thought is "I am ugly". Is this a description or an evaluation?

Most likely, this is an evaluation. Why? "Ugly" depends in the eye of the beholder, so to speak. Everybody has at least one ugly feature and at least one pretty feature. If you concentrate on the ugly feature, you will consider yourself to be ugly. Concentrate the beautiful features and you will feel beautiful.

For instance, there are people who look nice but will complain that they are ugly because "my nose is too big/small", "my teeth are crooked", "I don't like the color of my eyes", and so on.

Evaluations typically are harsh and puffed up. Restate your thoughts and turn into a factual description. This way, you know exactly what you can work on or improve or simply accept about yourself.

For example, you feel as if your nose is too big and it's making you look ugly. Is there a standard for nose size to be considered beautiful? None. Accept the nose size you have and realize that it is doing its function- helping you breathe. Stop stressing on how it looks.

"I am the worst public speaker". This is an evaluation, a judgment on your part.

Reword it into a description so you get the facts straight. This way, you get to declare what areas you need some work on and do just that. Descriptive statements also help you place your focus on reality and not be stressed about your harsh self-criticisms.

"I did not do well with my last presentation, particularly when presenting the problems. I was hesitant to go on for fear of offending someone at work."

That's a more descriptive way to do it and places your perspective on the more important things. This way, you do not beat yourself up for results you weren't happy with.

7. Rate believability

How much do you believe these negative self-thoughts? Probably 100% now and you are even unconsciously adding more credibility to it.

Take a step back and recall the times this self-thought came to mind. Rate how much you believed it each time it resurfaced. Probably there were times you believed in it 100%, sometimes 75%, sometimes 20% only.

This should make you realize that this particular negative self-thought is not absolute.

Next, rate the emotional pain or distress it creates. For example, today, you are thinking "I am a very bad presenter". How much emotional stress does this give you?

You might have a forthcoming big presentation at a board meeting, and you are presenting on behalf of your boss. That meeting will include most of the higher management. That could be giving you anxieties. At this point, the stress is already high for you. Then this negative self-thought surfaces. Its rate for emotional pain/distress is also high.

What to do?

Step back. Get back to the basics. You are nervous because the meeting is a big one and many important people will be there. You are presenting on behalf of your boss, so expectations are higher.

Your negative self-thoughts is brought about by an already existing stress.

This should make you realize that the negative self-thought is not a truth. It is rather an offshoot of current mental and emotional stress brought about by an event you are nervous about in the near future.

Believability changes. Emotional impact changes. Therefore, the negative self-thought is not an absolute truth about yourself. It is most likely biased. You have a choice and you can exercise control over these negative self-beliefs. Putting things into perspective is one step in dealing with these unhelpful beliefs.

Chapter 11: Improving Your Odds

Rome wasn't built in a day, and you are not going to be able to overcome mental weakness in a day, either. Whether you have certain strengths you need to enhance, or if you need to work on your entire mental strength overall, you are going to face challenges along the way. Remember, it is inevitable. If you feel that you are struggling to improve your strength in any of the skills from Chapter 3, this chapter will help you improve your odds and work toward your success with greater strength and optimism.

When Things Aren't Going Right, Right Now

There are many things that happen when you feel like things aren't going right. In general, these things are reflections of habits you are trying to let go of. Because of that, you may feel like even more of a failure, thus pushing you into a downward spiral of negative thoughts, limiting and dishonest beliefs, and overall struggle.

If you feel that things aren't going right and you are not achieving mental toughness, here are some symptoms you may notice in yourself:

- Negative self-talk
- Limiting and dishonest beliefs
- Lack of motivation
- Lowered emotional intelligence

- Overexerting yourself
- Not honoring your boundaries
- Lack of self-care
- Feelings of unworthiness, not embracing joy
- Dwelling on failure and anxiety
- Struggling to adapt to change
- Lack of self-confidence
- Being harshly affected by toxic people

As you may recognize, all of these symptoms tend to be going against what is required to be mentally tough. They also tend to be the common "reactions" we have when we feel that we are not seeing active success in our attempt to achieve our goals.

The very first thing you need to do when you feel as though you are not generating success in your attempt to build mental toughness is to go down this list and check off everything you are experiencing. If you are experiencing anything else, add that to your list as well. Developing this sense of self-awareness is the first step to getting back on track with your emotional intelligence. It is also the best way to discover all of the hidden ways that your psyche is working against you so that you can generate a plan to recognize these outdated behaviors and move past them. Be exhaustive in your list and seek to uncover all of the symptoms you are experiencing from your perceived failure, including all of the ones that seem to hide from plain sight, such as self-doubt, saying no to things that make you happy, or using language that asserts a lack of belief in yourself or your dreams.

Choose to Stay Positive

Once you have recognized all of these negative habits, there is one thing you have to do: make a choice. Choose to stay positive. When you consciously decide that you are going to choose positive thoughts and feelings over these obsessively negative ones, you are telling yourself that you **are** going to put in the effort to make a change, **period.** Not that you are thinking about it, or that you want to, or that you might "try". No, you are "**I will make this happen, no ifs, ands, or buts about it! I am going to succeed. Period.**" In fact, say it out loud with conviction. You **are** going to make this happen. You **are** a positive person. Failure is inevitable, and you have faced a little bit! Recall from Chapter 3, when you fail you must:

1. Recognize the "failure"
2. Reframe it into a lesson
3. Create an action-plan from that lesson
4. Act!

A fear of failure holds a lot of people back, so does a fear of success. However, when you think too much you achieve nothing, which brings us to our next point!

Focus on Action, Not Thought

Often we feel we are not advancing well because we are too consumed in thought.

This can lead to us wrongfully ignoring our advancements, **or** it can lead to us being too consumed by our thoughts to actually advance. For that reason, take that action plan that you made when you chose to stay positive and start acting. Stop thinking about whether you are making the right choices or not and just keep acting. Move forward a few steps first, and then stop to see where you can adjust your course and what you have learned until this point. Taking action immediately without thought and keeping this momentum up through at least a few steps in your action plan will help you feel as though you are making rapid progress toward your goal. Then, you can stop and slightly feed into your uncertainty by ensuring that you are on the right path and doing everything properly. If you see any opportunity for improvement, use this as your chance to adjust your course and move forward with a greater sense of clarity and direction. Then, every few steps forward, assess and adjust your course once more. Not only will this keep your momentum going, but it will also pull you out of your obsessive thoughts and keep you actively working toward your own success.

Ask for Help

If you are truly stumped or are feeling unsuccessful, ask for help! There are many ways that people can help you when it comes to building mental toughness and succeeding with your goals. You can ask anyone from a family member or friend to a counselor or a coach when it comes to getting help. You can also ask about any number of things that you may need help with. Perhaps you need someone to help you stay on track, or maybe you need someone to give you an outside perspective on your present situation. Or, maybe you just really need advice on overcoming a certain part of the obstacle that you can't seem to overcome on your own.

Regardless of what you need help with, never be afraid to ask for help. No matter what the subject is, there are always people out there prepared to help you. There are also countless platforms you can ask for help on. Here are some ideas, in case you're stuck:

- Online forums
- Coaches (e.g. life coaches, sports coaches, business coaches)
- Counselors or psychologists
- Friends
- Family members
- Coworkers
- Fellow entrepreneurs
- A community member
- A church member or religious figure (e.g. your chosen deity)
- Search engine searches
- A librarian (who can recommend a book on said subject)

There are many resources that you can tap into when you are looking for help on any given subject. Never be afraid to ask, no matter who you are asking for help. You will always be able to find someone who can give you the answer you need in order to continue moving forward.

Assess Your Environment

Something many people overlook is their physical environment. Often, we try to develop new skills but we do not create an optimal environment for us to do so. For example, perhaps you want to increase your tolerance and neutralize the way toxic people affect you. However, you practice by throwing yourself into a very intense situation with highly toxic people that you have struggled to deal with for a long time, assuming that this time you would be able to do it differently. Even though you may have psyched yourself up, practiced in the mirror, and planned out how you were going to be different this time, it is likely that you are not going to succeed in this type of circumstance. Habit will almost always take over when you are feeling afraid and cause for you to act in your usual ways.

Rather than throwing yourself in the fire and expecting yourself to improve overnight, take your time. Acclimate yourself by starting with easier situations and working your way up. Eventually you will find that you are able to handle the much more difficult situations with ease. As well, this route will get you toward success much faster than simply throwing yourself in the flame and expecting yourself not to burn.

Chapter 12: Business

Developing a tough mentality in business requires years of experience. If you happen to lose an investment, take it as an opportunity to learn. Learn from your mistakes. Study different business structures and how they became successful and why some businesses fail.

Success in business is also a matter of luck and proper timing. Also, come up with different contingency plans. You will never know when they will come in handy. Remember that mental toughness in business is being prepared mentally and financially. The next time you engage in the business, you'll know what to do.

Define your goals and know your priorities. What exactly are your business goals? Is it about giving jobs and opportunities to people? Is it about introducing into society a product that will solve a certain industrial problem? As mentioned earlier, defining your goals is important since you will incorporate these goals into your everyday activities. Moreover, classify your goals according to short-term and long term goals for this will help you achieve your success little by little.

Approach your problems one at a time. Just be steady and slow. You aren't a superhuman. If you try to solve all your problems in just one sitting, you might probably end up with a new problem. Know yourself more and learn your pacing.

Learn to be committed and dedicated. When your plans fail, don't be discouraged to get up and try again. Failures are part of life. Bill Gates, Warren Buffet and others did not succeed on their first try. Now that you know what doesn't work, incorporate them next into your business proposals and implementations and you'll definitely have more positive results.

Chapter 13: Mindfulness

People have all kinds of ideas when they hear the word "mindfulness." What does it mean and how does it affect how mentally tough you are? Well, it helps you to see the bigger picture but to do so in a calm and composed way. Imagine two bosses. One is always stressed and passes that stress on to his staff. He has a short temper and is hated by people who work for him. Then you have people like Richard Branson – the Virgin millionaire. He is someone that employees really enjoy working for. He lets people think and take their time being aware of the processes that make up the working day. How do you think that such a difference exists? It's called mental toughness. Richard Branson is in tune with his body and with the world around him. The rest is history. You too can be like this if you realize what it means to be present in your life. Many people make the mistake of worrying about things and panicking. However, when you introduce mindfulness into your life, there's no rush anymore. You are totally aware of what you are doing at any given time and do it with all your heart, thus being able to complete things quicker.

Being mindful starts with how you view the world. Do you get up in the morning and dread the day? Do you get up worrying about stuff that happened yesterday? Mindful people have chosen to drop this baggage and enjoy the sensation of being in the present moment. They wake, and they look at the state of the sky. They taste their morning coffee and enjoy it. The reason that the human body has senses is so that people can be more aware. If you ignore those senses, you become less able to exercise mental toughness. Let's give you some examples of people who don't use mindfulness.

- Katy is late every day for work. She races through traffic and doesn't notice anything around her.

- Mike always eats his sandwiches while he is working. If you were to ask him five minutes later what he ate, chances are he wasn't even aware of eating it, let alone appreciating tastes.

- Sam always worries about things she says to people. Her mind lives in the past and is so busy digesting things that have happened that she doesn't have time to be in the now.

I could give you a million examples of things that people do that take them away from the present moment, but to practice mindfulness, you need to sit somewhere quietly and become aware of something as simple as your breath. Breathe in through the nostrils to the count of 7 and then breathe out to the count of 9 trying all the time to only think about your breathing. When you breathe, if you think of other things, simply acknowledge them, and then cut off those thoughts because they are taking away your ability to be mindful. Do this for several moments a couple of times a day and you will become mentally tough and able to deal with things you may never have been able to deal with in the past.

Do not judge people, thoughts or things; allow everything to be, just as it is. If you practice this on a regular basis, what you are doing is allowing your mind to digest things in a better manner. Your mind will be quieter, and you can deal with problems in a much more effective way. You will find that if you stop being impulsive and start to find answers within yourself, those who are not mentally tough may not have thought about. The reason? You let your mind do what it is supposed to do. You became mindful.

If you find yourself living in a moment that isn't this moment, try to step into the now. The more you train yourself, the better you will be able to do it. Remember, you were given senses for a good reason. Use them and bring yourself back to the present moment. If things start to go through your mind, acknowledge them but don't give way to anything that doesn't relate to now. Instead, simply come back to this moment, using breathing, smelling, tasting, touching and seeing. You'd be surprised how much people miss in their lives because they are not mentally tough enough to see it. When you take away judgment, you slow your mind down sufficiently to be able to tackle problems. Have you ever answered someone in a hasty manner and regretted what you said? Most people have, but only because they don't know how to still their minds. They feel their options are limited and must let the words come out of their mouths. However, now think of this. Someone says something that would normally offend and upset you. You let the thought go and you come back into the moment. You don't judge what has been said, but merely see it like a moment that happened and has now gone. In other words, you act in a mentally tough way and face the problem as and when you feel that it's relevant to what you are doing.

People will gain more respect for you if you can deal with life in this manner.

When you have a job to do, switch off all outside interference and give everything you have to that job. Use a timer if you want to and tell yourself that you will devote 35 minutes to just that job. Don't think about other things. Don't even talk to people. What you are doing is allowing yourself the space you need to get things done and that's the best way forward. The message you send to others is that you are mentally tough but fair and can be trusted to do things right. Take a break and then time yourself for another 35 minutes of uninterrupted work and you will get twice as much done as the man who sits at his desk and mulls over something that happened last night.

This moment should be the only one that counts. It's a little difficult at first to do this, so you will need to practice bringing yourself back to the moment. Associate different events in your life with what your senses feel. An aroma may make you think of someone you like. These are good and positive associations, but they link things that are worthwhile. Mentally tough people can do this. I remember dealing with a child when Haiti was devastated by natural disaster. One very mentally tough child picked a daisy and associated it with what she was aiming for in her life and smiled. I asked her why she smiled when so much around her was devastated. Her answer was wonderful. "Because I can," she said, as she proceeded to make her sister a daisy chain. She was one mentally tough young lady. She was in the moment and even though the moment offered her very little in the way of a future, was able to see beyond it and find something positive in the NOW that no one could take away from her.

Chapter 14: The Discipline Of Will And Its Types

Kindness and virtue

In Stoicism, for every virtue we seek, there is a corresponding vice that you need to uproot. The objective is to replace vice with virtue. Now, you and I started this journey because you want to live the good life. We have defined what the good life is from a Stoic perspective. One crucial element of this life is maintaining harmony with the universe. I did this quick trip back to the beginning to bring us into focus because humility is something many of us struggle with. I have heard people question the purpose of humility. We think it is a quality that keeps us in the gutter with people we consider undesirables. But without humility, you may never be able to get out of your comfort zone. For too long, we have identified fear as the primary reason many of us want to stay where we are, and yes, fear can hold us back. But ego is what makes you stagnant. When you start to think you know it all, you have it all, you create chains that anchor you to that spot in life. To break those chains, spend your mornings meditating on scenes guided by the following thought processes:

1. *See your death vividly*. I read about a group of early Stoics who would occasionally hold a feast in the presence of a corpse. This is insane, just as the thought of seeing your death, but only if you are missing the point. And the point here is to find the

answer to this question. How big is your ego going to be when you are six feet under? Nobody looks at a corpse and marvels at its intelligence or how wealthy it was. The best quality that can be attributed to a corpse is that it looks "restful," and not even the artistic skills of the best mortician can change this. Despite the commonly-held belief in an afterlife, your influence over the living ceases the day you die. The effect of death on the body of a rich, influential person is exactly the same on that of a poor nobody. Death, which is the conclusive end of all things, pays no attention to things that make you think that you are better than everyone. Instead of pondering on those superficial things that feed your ego, meditate on your death and recognize that, in the end, none of those things matter—everyone meets the same end.

2. ***Acknowledge that tomorrow is not guaranteed***. If you are one of those people who loves to procrastinate, meditating on this could help you be more proactive. If you are also struggling with your relationships, this meditation exercise can help bring things into perspective. We have a tendency to take things for granted. We abuse the grace of waking up to see each day. We don't appreciate those in our lives, because we take their presence for granted. What would you regret the most if you died right now? If you can do something about it now, do it and stop putting it off. Tell those you care about how much you appreciate them.

In some books, this is referred to as self-discipline or self-control. In life, we are almost always in a constant state of want. And, more often than not, our wants are not always the same as our needs. Our carnality is propelled by what books like the Bible refer to as the "desires of the flesh."

The entire sales force in the world is built on this concept. You turn on the TV to see a nice-looking guy running and, without so many words, you are programmed to think that to get that body, you need to run— and for your running to feel good, you need the shoes he is wearing. This prompting of your desire is so strong that even if you have 10 sports shoes lined up in the back of your closet, you still feel you need this one shoe.

This kind of feeling is amplified in areas of our lives that have to do with gratifying our pleasure impulses. This virtue is all about tempering those instincts that drive our wants. It is, in essence, the application of wisdom when dealing with temptations.

Amor fati/ acceptance

Fate is a dangerous concept. The idea that certain events in our lives are predestined to happen is something we all struggle with. It makes us feel powerless in our bid to change the events that dictate our daily experience, and even when we come to a place of acceptance, we do so with dejection, sadness, and a "why me" attitude. Now, when I am talking about fate, I am not referring to what you had for breakfast—no, you were not fated to eat cereal this morning. Things like breakfast are within your control because you had a choice in the matter. A diagnosis of something you dreadful that you least expected, that is fate. Winning the Powerball lottery on your first attempt also involves the hand of fate. Basically, anything that happens to you without your choice in the matter is fate. Although there are exceptions, fate does not need your permission.

In line with today's double-standard custom, we tend to celebrate fate when it favors us. We don't question the abundant blessings we receive, even when we know we did not do anything to earn or deserve it. The moment things go awry, however, we get upset. These ill-fated setbacks drive us into an emotional downward spiral that we may never truly recover from. Many of us have made several attempts to fight fate. This rebellion sets us on a path that clearly has no end, yet we totally commit ourselves to it in the hope that, somehow, we can thwart fate. After wasting so much time and energy, we come to a place where we finally give in and surrender— except more often than not, we come to this realization a little too late, or after we have wasted so much time and resources trying to avoid what should have been embraced from the beginning.

Now, I'm not saying you should roll over and play dead when something you did not predict happens to you or the people you love. That would be ridiculous advice. But a scene from a very popular medical TV series often comes to my mind when I think of fate, and I believe that this is the best illustration for the point I am trying to make.

In this scene, there was a single dad who came to the hospital with his terminally ill daughter. This ailment was diagnosed from the time that this child was a baby and they had been managing her care ever since. However, the child suffered a major health crisis in this scene and according to the doctors, there was nothing else that could be medically done to improve things for her. In fact, they did not think she would make it through the night. The concerned dad understandably refused to accept the damning verdict. Instead, he raced out, leaving his daughter in the care of physicians while he made a mad dash to spring for a cure. He was out of money, out of time, and out of ideas, but he was willing to try anything that could offer the possibility of saving his young daughter's life. Naturally, it was heartbreaking. For a parent, it is instinctive to want to protect your child and he just followed his instinct, but in doing so, he nearly missed out on a moment he would never have been able to forgive himself for missing. So, if this moment was important to him, why was he out there fighting it? Because he did not embrace fate.

We are groomed to expect miracles, and while miracles are known to happen, they also fall within the realm of things we do not control. You cannot manipulate a miracle, just like you cannot manipulate fate. But in embracing fate, you don't take on the dormant role, even though it may feel like it.

The fire is your potential. Obstacles, challenges, and fate's whims are the things that are thrown into the fire. Your decision not to embrace these things will not stop them from happening to you. As a matter of fact, you might see the embers of your potential burning out faster because you are unable to bring yourself to a place of acceptance.

I have a few mental exercises that will help awaken a mindset within you that embraces this Stoic philosophy:

1. *Be balanced in your thinking.* When things happen to you, good or bad, train yourself not to react emotionally. While your instincts may be self-serving, they don't always serve a higher good. Think rationally and objectively, and let your actions be guided by this. During your thinking

167

process, assess the situation by weighing in on the dangers and risks that threaten your objective. Ask the right questions that would provide solutions to those risks you listed out, then act accordingly.

2. ***Get comfortable with being uncomfortable.*** Since you have accepted that you cannot change what has happened, ask yourself how you can make it work to your advantage. This exercise is particularly good for people who have suffered some kind of trauma. Tragic as it was, it has already happened. There is no going back, no undoing, and certainly no forgetting. But you have a choice: accept it and redefine your experience, or fight it and let it control your experience. You've heard the expression, "If life gives you lemons, make lemonade." This just means to make the best of your situation. I remember losing a close friend of mine and, yes, his death was

painful. I was racked with grief and couldn't function for days. But as I reflected on his life, I came to the realization that I could either celebrate his life—which was glorious—or wallow in his death. I chose life, and even though it still hurts to not have him here, I can find joy in the knowledge that I was privileged to know this amazing person.

This is the most important of the Stoic virtues and it refers to our ability to discern good from the bad. It is believed that wisdom is the only virtue, while the remaining three cardinal virtues which we will discuss shortly are simply its primary applications. Seeing that wisdom is essentially practical reasoning, I tend to agree with that thinking.

Wisdom is the foundation of all Stoic logic, because you cannot make sound decisions and actions if you have no clear understanding of what is good and what is bad. In this application, good does not refer to what appeals to the senses. The smell of a nice, warm bowl of soup can be very appealing to whoever perceives it, but that does not automatically ascribe the moral value of good to it. The bowl of soup falls under the preferred indifferent category. Eating this bowl of soup will not make you a good person or a terrible person, it is how you go about your pursuit of the soup—whether you steal it or cook it—that is classified as either good or bad.

Wisdom is the understanding of the true nature of good. With this understanding, you are able to ascribe value to different external things rationally. Under Stoic teachings, a wise person is not just someone who can tell the difference between good and bad. For a person to call himself wise, he must be able to offer himself wise counsel. In other words, wisdom is an internalized process.

Resilience and Fortitude

Fear is another prominent driving emotion behind most of our decisions. You find people who work themselves to the bones because they are afraid of not being able to afford the things they want. They sometimes live a stagnant and unprogressive life, deliberately avoiding risks that would propel them forward, even if those risks are supported by their rational thinking or wisdom.

This virtue grants the ability to act on the wisdom you have discerned, even if it is not exactly conventional. Wisdom is fantastic, but without the application of wisdom, it is just another nice thing something thought or said. This virtue is also likened to endurance. But in that sad, long-suffering way that makes you a victim of circumstance. But in an emboldened form that sees you facing down your deepest fears and not acting on them. Rather, you push past it to think and act logically. You can say fortitude is wisdom applied in adversity.

Stoicism on mortality and the Key to Living Fully

Again, this is an area where we have issues with the direct translation of the word. When you hear justice, you may think this refers to the legal sense of the word, but that definition is simply not enough to encapsulate the true Stoic reference of this virtue. While an aspect of this virtue implies a state where we are obedient to the laws of the land, it goes much deeper than this.

Morality, on the other hand, does not fully encompass the stoic meaning of the word, either. In this instance, we are talking about doing right or, as some people would like to say, living an upright life. If you are the religious sort, you may go as far as calling it righteousness. However, between morality and justice, we can understand what this virtue is about.

In practical terms, justice or morality is the application of wisdom in social interactions. We've established that wisdom is the knowledge of good and bad, and the ability to clearly distinguish between both. It is one thing to know something, it is another thing to act on it. In your dealings with people, justice/morality refers to the wisdom you apply in relating to them. Your respect and treatment of others are not based on their status, gender, or the benefits they offer. Rather, you make a deliberate choice to be fair and impartial.

Chapter 15: Cultivating Mental Toughness Among Employees

In the issue of corporate affairs, entrepreneurs know that of all the elements in their companies, the hardest to reproduce are their employees. Therefore, they must make every effort to maintain this factor, and the leaders must do all that they can to ensure that the teams are supported in their roles, emotionally, physically, and mentally. They must also be well.

An American university came up with a model for mental toughness, which showed that people who do show signs of mental toughness are likely to do well at their work. The data from the study indicated that these people are much more successful, have a commendable record of accomplishment, and are mostly the ones who hold leadership positions in the companies. They also tend to be competitive, driven, and ambitious in their dealing. A mentally strong person will also be open to challenges and changes in his working environment.

If you think about the occupants of a regular boardroom, you are likely to agree that many people in there fall into the category of the mentally tough irrespective of the departments they represent. However, you will find that these executives represent a combination of mentally strong and sensitive employees. The sensitive employees are not weak though. A sensitive person has a mix of desirable attitudes and skills, but he finds assessment and transitions quite tricky.

Sensitive workers need targeted support to increase their resilience and ability to handle challenges. It is important to note that while mentally tough people develop their resilience from overcoming failures and moving on swiftly without letting anything deter their performance. Sensitive people, on the other hand, are motivated by success. Once a sensitive person can achieve success after overcoming one challenge, he or she is confident that he or she can overcome the next one.

Sensitive employees need to learn the skills of mentally tough people to develop mental toughness. They should learn that maintaining their ground even during tough times would grant them the confidence they need to keep composure during tough times. It is all right to be emotional, but exercising some level of control over them is of benefit. When you are in control, you will not just give an emotional response driven by your fear and discomfort; you will check your emotions and proceed with the business of the day in a calm manner.

Teaching mental toughness can be quite a task, and it is not certain that employees would even be interested in attending the classes. However, research and experience show that behavior is better learned and adapted when modeled. As such, here is how you can model mental toughness and resilience among your staff.

Become the example: Mental toughness should be modeled right from the top. A leader should lead by example. If he wants his employees to learn how not to freak out and to rise to the occasion when challenges come, then he ought to model that too. Looking at it from a family angle, the leader being the father or the mother, and the children being the followers, it would be impossible for the children to remain strong when their parent is shivering in fright at a corner. However, once you show your child how to show bravery even when the situation is frightening, then the child will learn to be brave. The employees read and borrow from the attitude of their boss.

Promote confidence and control among the staff: No one would feel confident if, at the least sign of trouble, troops are sent over to come to offer help. It would be impossible for employees to become mentally tough if the management is always hovering around them to provide help. Employees who have a sense of control over what they do become mentally tough because they have learned to face challenges head-on, take ownership of their mistakes, and to take the glory when they achieve success.

Nurture a sense of purpose in your staff: A leader or an employer nurtures a sense of purpose by encouraging his employees to look for meaning and purpose in whatever they are doing. When employees feel that what they do has some significance in the world, they are likely to be more vested in their work

Address the levels and the causes of stress in the workplace. Employees experience stress both as a group and as individuals. The management needs to be aware of that. Therefore, the management should be on the lookout for when tensions are rising for the group and come up with a solution for them. As individuals, the management needs to keep track of each person's performance, and attendance records, among other factors, to identify stress in individuals.

Encourage networking among the employees: The establishment of networks and connections among the people fosters an environment of support that helps to nurture mental toughness by providing each employee with people who can help encourage and build them when tough times come.

Manage change effectively: Leaders and employers should ensure that the entire workforce understands the need for change at one time or another. Change should be a welcome challenge rather than a roadblock. Change can happen in any environment, and mentally tough employees can adapt easier than others do.

Nurture resilience: Resilience is an element of mental toughness. It should be a critical point of focus among employees because it keeps them from giving up when the situation becomes tough. Instead of providing solutions every time, an employee should be left to strive with the challenge on their hands until he finds a solution. Avoid providing assistance all the time, lest the employees become too dependent on you. The more an employee struggles and overcomes, the stronger the resilience and mental toughness in him, and in the entire organization.

Treasure a sense of humor: Encourage employees to laugh and be happy throughout their working day. Happiness cancels out the stress that challenges present, and if the employee can keep his mind off the worry, he will be able to come up with a solution sooner. The employee will be able to walk through the challenges without having to break down.

Provide learning opportunities: Learning expands the mind and provides the opportunity for developing professionally. Occasionally, employees should have opportunities to be taught and learning. It is by increasing their knowledge that they learn how to manage themselves through tough situations and to embrace change.

Embrace optimism: Creating a positive, optimistic environment means that you adopt a positive language. Optimism encourages mental toughness by keeping the people from losing heart even when the challenge intensifies. On the other hand, if employees have to suffer through negative language and discouragement, they are likely to have a negative attitude in their work and to give up early when issues arise. The leadership will be at a loss because the turnover rate will rise.

Encourage the employees to become adaptable and flexible: When employees are flexible, they are less likely to crumble when pressure mounts. At a time of intense pressure, they are likely to find creative ways of pushing through the challenges until they overcome.

Make use of the employees' skills of managing and resolving problems. Both the leadership and the staff have some problem-solving ideas and skills that can be taken up to neutralize the issues and their effects. Companies who take this approach towards resolving issues, taking the input of everyone in the organization, have a history of successfully implementing solutions and growing the toughness, resilience, and independence of their employees.

In the corporate world, it is important to remember that tough times do not last, it is the tough people that do. Always yearn to develop mental toughness among your staff because they are the real assets of your company. If they are tough, whatever the situation that comes up, you and your company will be left standing. It is also easier to rebuild if systems come crashing down.

Key Elements to Building Your Employees' Mental Strength

1. Foster the spirit of community within the organization

No one likes to be alone all the time, especially when others are socializing and getting along. The act of positioning an employee to feel like part of the larger group effectively counteracts loneliness, which can overwhelm a person's mind and keep him from thinking clearly. One researcher observed that lonely people are less likely to receive awards than those who are social. This could also mean that they are less productive than those who engage with others and get to learn about different ways to approach a problem.

In your place of work, you ought to encourage the community spirit by coming up with groups that can help employees relate to each other even beyond the issues that have to do with work. For example, you could create a support group for people who want to quit drinking and smoking, in addition to the establishment of a mentorship program. This way, people will be caring for each other and supporting each other, and with regard for every member.

2. Take up hiring processes that are of benefit to the candidates as much as they are to you

Use a method that will help the candidates realize whether the job matches their likes and preferences and whether they will do the job out of passion or simply to have an occupation. In our job searches, many of us are quite desperate and will send thousands of applications, to see if any company will have a place for us. It is impossible for a human being to be passionate about what a thousand companies are doing. If you end up taking a role that you are not excited about, you are likely to break under the weight of the stress, pressure, and the challenges that come about.

For this reason, the hiring method ought to benefit both the hiring company and the applicant so that each may identify the right fit. It saves both parties a lot of time and energy. As an employee, you end up doing what you like or were meant to do. If you find a role like this one, you will not have to be encouraged or pushed by anyone. You will love challenges and will be overwhelmed by the thrill of accomplishment and beating them down.

Therefore, as an employer, ensure that you only take in like-minded employees, those with whom you share a passion for what you do.

3. Focus on building physical strength too, in addition to psychological strength

The first thing that wears down a strong mind is physical fatigue, sickness, and generally feeling worn out. Physical wellness requires that you maintain a healthy diet and that you exercise often. Leaders have to proactively take care of these issues by providing these structures, either physically at the workplaces, or through allowances that will allow the employees to afford these amenities. For example, some workplaces have gyms within the job premises where members can go before or after the day's work.

Others register their members to private gyms and then issues them with cards. Whichever strategy an organization takes up, the end game should be to boost the physical wellness of the staff.